Start TO finish
Second Series

Food

FROM
Peanut TO Peanut Butter

ROBIN NELSON

LERNER PUBLICATIONS COMPANY Minneapolis

Lerner Publications Company
A division of Lerner Publishing Group, Inc.
241 First Avenue North
Minneapolis, MN 55401 U.S.A.

Website address: www.lernerbooks.com

Photo Acknowledgments
The images in this book are used with the permission of: © Gary Woodard/Dreamstime.com; © Photoeuphoria/Dreamstime.com, p. 3; Georgia Peanut Commission, pp. 5, 9, 21; © Louise McKerchar/American Peanut Council, pp. 7, 11, 13; © Pert Laboratories, p. 15; Courtesy of SUPERVALU Inc., pp. 17, 19; © Todd Strand/Independent Picture Service, p. 23.

Front cover: © Karen Sarraga/Dreamstime.com.

Main body text set in Arta Std Book 20/26.
Typeface provided by International Typeface Corp.

Library of Congress Cataloging-in-Publication Data

Nelson, Robin, 1971–
     From peanut to peanut butter / by Robin Nelson.
          p.   cm. — (Start to finish, second series. food)
     Includes index.
     ISBN 978–0–7613–9180–7 (lib. bdg. : alk. paper)
     1. Peanut butter—Juvenile literature. 2. Peanuts—Processing—Juvenile literature. I. Title.
TP438.P4N454 2013
641.3'56596—dc23   2011036511

Manufactured in the United States of America
1 – DP – 7/15/12

Table of Contents

Peanut butter tastes good! How is it made?

A farmer grows peanuts.

A farmer plants peanut seeds. The seeds grow into peanut plants. Little buds called **pegs** grow on the plants. The pegs push into the ground and grow under the dirt. The pegs become peanuts.

The sun dries the peanuts.

The farmer uses a digging machine to dig up the peanut plants. The peanuts are wet and dirty. A shaking machine shakes the dirt off the peanuts. The peanut plants are spread on the ground to dry in the sun for a few days.

The peanuts are picked up.

A farmer uses a machine called a **combine** to pick up the peanut plants. The combine puts the peanuts in a large box. Then it pulls the peanuts off the plants.

The peanuts are sorted.

Trucks take the peanuts to a **shelling factory**. A shelling factory is a place where peanuts are sorted and cleaned. Workers sort the peanuts by size. Small peanuts are used to make peanut butter.

Machines remove the shells.

A shelling machine pushes the peanuts through small holes in a piece of metal. The shells are crushed. A fan blows the shells away.

Workers check the peanuts.

Workers check the peanuts. Peanuts that are not good to eat are removed. The good peanuts are poured into bags. The bags are sent to a factory to be made into peanut butter.

The peanuts are cooked.

The peanuts are put into big ovens.
The ovens cook the peanuts. Cooking
the peanuts makes them taste better.

Machines mix the peanut butter.

Machines crush the peanuts into very small pieces. Vegetable oil and salt are mixed in. Sometimes sugar or honey is added. Machines mix the peanut butter until it is smooth.

The peanut butter is put into jars.

A machine called a **filler** squirts the peanut butter into empty jars. Another machine puts lids on the jars. Trucks take the peanut butter to stores to be sold.

Peanut butter makes a great snack.

You can spread peanut butter on bread or eat it with celery. You can even eat it right out of the jar!

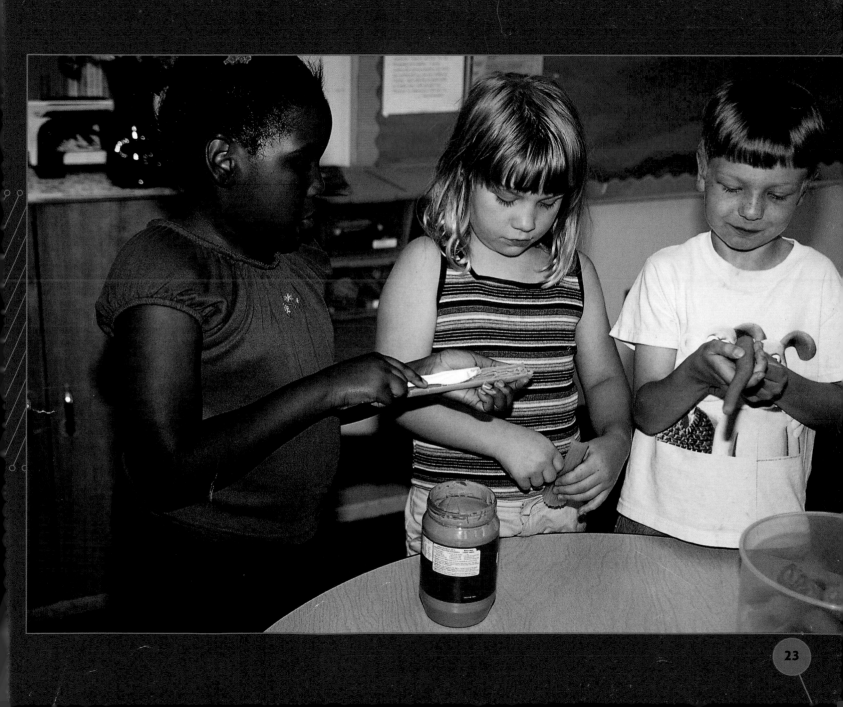

Glossary

combine (KAHM-byn): a machine that collects and cleans peanuts

filler (FIHL-ur): a machine that squirts peanut butter into jars

pegs (PEHGZ): the buds of a peanut plant

shelling factory (SHEHL-ing FAK-tur-ee): a place where peanuts are cleaned and sorted

Index

LERNER

SOURCE

Expand learning beyond the printed book. Download free, complementary educational resources for this book from our website, www.lernerresource.com.